Science and Technology
Cars and Motorcycles

John Townsend

Chicago, Illinois

www.heinemannraintree.com
Visit our website to find out
more information about
Heinemann-Raintree books.

To order:

☎ Phone 888-454-2279

🖥 Visit www.heinemannraintree.com
to browse our catalog and order online.

© 2012 Raintree
an imprint of Capstone Global Library, LLC
Chicago, Illinois

Edited by Andrew Farrow, Adam Miller, and Diyan Leake
Designed by Victoria Allen
Original illustrations © Capstone Global Library Ltd 2012
Illustrated by Oxford Designers and Illustrators
Picture research by Elizabeth Alexander
Originated by Capstone Global Library
Printed and bound in China by CTPS

15 14 13 12
10 9 8 7 6 5 4 3 2

Library of Congress Cataloging-in-Publication Data
Townsend, John, 1955-
   Cars and motorcycles / John Townsend.
      p. cm.—(Sci-hi. Science and technology)
   Includes bibliographical references and index.
   ISBN 978-1-4109-4269-2 (hc)—ISBN 978-1-4109-4278-4
(pb) 1. Automobiles—Dynamics—Juvenile literature.
2. Motorcycles—Dynamics—Juvenile literature. 3.
Automobiles—Design and construction—Juvenile
literature. 4. Motorcycles—Design and construction—
Juvenile literature. I. Title.
   TL243.T695 2012
   629.2'31—dc22   2010054317

Acknowledgments
The author and publishers are grateful to the following
for permission to reproduce copyright material:
Alamy pp. **10** (© PhotoStockFile), **14**, **15**, **22**
(© culture-images GmbH), **23** (© idp oulton park
collection), **24** (© Bob Weymouth); BUB Enterprises
2009 © WWW.bub.com p. **33**; Corbis pp. **9** (© George
Tiedemann/NewSport), **13** (© Marc Sanchez/Icon
SMI), **16**, **17** (© Handout/Reuters), **19** (© PCN), **30** (©
Car Culture), **35** (© Lee Sanders/epa), **34** (© Toshiyuki
Aizawa/Reuters), **37** (© Michael Crabtree/Reuters), **38**
(© Kevin Bartram/Reuters); Getty Images pp. **29** (Junko
Kimura), **31** (Johanna Leguerre/AFP), **36** (© 2009 John
Kosak); Getty Images for NASCAR p. **7** (John Harrelson);
PA Photos p. **32** (GetPress/ABACA USA/Empics
Entertainment); Photolibrary pp. **4** (Axel Schmies), **5**
(Novastock), **6** (Dan Barba), **11** (Javier Larrea), **28** (Anton
Luhr); Press Association Images p. **26** (© 2009 Press
Association/Sutton/Sutton Motorsport); Shutterstock
pp. **18** (© Walter G Arce), **20**, **contents page** top (©
Daniel Gangur), **21**, **contents page** bottom (© Harsányi
András), **all background and design features**.

Main cover photograph of Caparo T1 supercar,
reproduced with permission of Rex Features
(Geoff Moore); inset cover photograph of inflatable
balloon reproduced with permission of shutterstock
(© Daniel Gangur).

The publisher would like to thank literary consultant
Nancy Harris and content consultant Suzy Gazlay for
their assistance in the preparation of this book.

Contents

How does friction help drivers? Find out on page 20!

Why do bikers lean into a bend? Turn to page 21 to find out!

Some words are shown in bold, **like this**. These words are explained in the glossary. You will find important information and definitions underlined, <u>like this</u>.

SCIENCE ON WHEELS

What would the world be like without cars and motorcycles? It is difficult to imagine, but these machines have only been around for a very short part of our history. The invention of the modern engine has totally changed the world we live in.

Amazing technology

Today, we expect a car or motorcycle to spring into life at the turn of a key. Hundreds of moving parts all smoothly work together to turn the wheels. We probably don't think about all the powerful technology at work. Amazing science makes cars and motorcycles the remarkable machines they are today.

INTERNAL COMBUSTION ENGINES

The internal combustion (burning) engine creates heat energy (the ability to do work) to make vehicles move. It burns fuel and oxygen within the engine itself. This was new science in the 1880s. At that time, steam engines used the heat from a separate fire. This was external (outside) combustion.

In 1886, Gottlieb Daimler (1834–1900) of Germany made the world's first gasoline-powered motorcycle. He built it by strapping a combustion engine to a wooden bicycle.

Progress

The world's first vehicles with wheels were invented by farmers in Central Asia. Tiny models of their two-wheeled carts pulled by camels and bulls have been found from 5,000 to 6,000 years ago. But it is only in the last 100 years or so that people have been able to drive vehicles without "animal power." At the start of the 1900s, designers called **engineers** finally developed **mass-produced** vehicles (vehicles produced in large quantities). This made it possible for people to move around quickly and comfortably.

The internal combustion engine led to all kinds of sports, such as motorcycle racing.

FORCE

All kinds of **forces** are at work on our planet. <u>A force is something that pulls or pushes objects to make them move, speed up, slow down, change direction, or change shape.</u> Such forces are at work whenever a car or motorcycle drives off.

Moving force

You are sitting in the driver's seat of a car. The engine is running, you release the brakes, and the car moves forward. Simple! But one of the big questions that puzzled scientists for years was: "How do things move—and why?"

Three hundred years ago, the great English scientist Isaac Newton (1642–1727) came up with answers. They are now known as Newton's Laws of Motion. They help to explain why today's vehicles get moving, keep moving, and stop.

Newton's Laws of Motion explain the action of modern rocket-powered cars.

Newton's Laws of Motion

- <u>A still object will remain still unless it is pulled or pushed by a force</u>. It will then keep moving at the same speed in the same direction—unless another force acts on it. In other words, a motorcycle needs a force to make it go. It will keep going in a straight line unless another force (such as **friction**, a rubbing force from brakes) slows it down or makes it turn.

- <u>For an object to move faster, it needs greater force</u>. Heavier objects need more force to make them gain speed than lighter objects. So, a lightweight motorcycle will speed up faster than a bus full of people.

- <u>For every action, there is an equal and opposite reaction</u>. This means if an object is being pushed along, it is also pushing back just as hard. So, a rocket engine pushes out burning gases backward with great force, but an equal force pushes the rocket forward.

KEY SCIENCE

If things are to move, they need energy. The energy that keeps things moving is called kinetic energy.

The Laws of Motion make for some dramatic car races!

BLAST FORCE

As the driving force of a car or motorcycle, the engine must release energy. A combustion engine gets its energy from burning fuel (gasoline, diesel, or **biofuel**, which is made from plants or animal waste). Fire makes cars and motorcycles work. As tiny sprays of fuel squirt into an engine, they are lit by electric sparks and—BOOM! Every second, hundreds of mini-explosions push down **pistons**, which are parts that are connected to rods. The rods drive a part called a **crankshaft**. The crankshaft is connected to the part of the engine that drives the car's wheels.

This usually happens in four quick stages (see the diagram below).

- A piston moves down to take a mixture of fuel and air into a **cylinder** (a tube-shaped part of the engine).
- This mix is **compressed** (squeezed) by the piston pushing back up.
- A spark ignites (explodes) the fuel, which pushes the piston back down.
- The piston moves up again, pushing out the burned gases. These are called **exhaust** gases.

This type of engine is a **four-stroke engine**. The "four" refers to the number of times a piston moves up and down to complete one cycle.

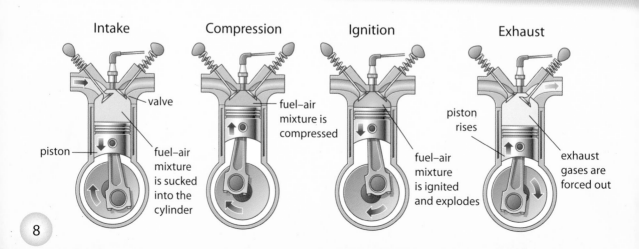

Intake | Compression | Ignition | Exhaust

valve

piston — | fuel–air mixture is sucked into the cylinder | fuel–air mixture is compressed | piston rises | fuel–air mixture is ignited and explodes | exhaust gases are forced out

Keeping cool

With all this combustion going on, engines get very hot. Sometimes they reach sizzling temperatures of about 2,000 degrees Celsius (°C), or 3,600 degrees Fahrenheit (°F). They must be cooled, or they would melt or burst into flames.

There are three ways to cool an engine:

- Liquid cooling: Water flows through pipes in an engine, carrying heat away to be cooled by a part called the radiator.

- Air cooling: The cylinders often have fins on their outsides, which are cooled by air blowing through them.

- **Lubrication**: Oil keeps engine parts moving smoothly, to reduce heat from friction.

Without flowing water, air, and oil, a combustion engine would soon overheat or explode.

ENVIRONMENTAL IMPACT

Some motorcycles have an engine that completes the piston cycle in two strokes. This can be lighter and more powerful than a four-stroke engine. But it is often noisier and dirtier.

The heat is on when a race car's cooling system fails to cope.

Torque

You may have heard drivers or engineers talk about **torque**. But what is it? <u>Torque is something like "a turning force."</u> The amount of torque an engine has will affect a car's **performance** (ability to speed up) and its ability to push itself along.

ALL TORQUE

• If you use a wrench to tighten a bolt, you are applying a sort of turning force.

• The longer the wrench, the greater the torque.

• The greater an engine's torque, the more turning force it can apply to the wheels.

A jeep needs high torque to climb a steep slope like this.

Changing gears

Have you ever wondered why some drivers need to change **gears** all the time? (This is only true for some cars. In automatic cars, the car does it for the driver.) Gears help increase or decrease the "turning force," or torque, of an engine. This means that changing gear will change the torque. So, when a car or motorcycle is climbing a steep hill, the driver changes to a lower gear (first or second). This increases the torque and makes the wheels turn more slowly, to move the vehicle uphill.

A higher gear

It takes great force to get a car moving. Gears can greatly increase the torque required for starting to move. The gears reduce the speed of the engine, but they increase its "turning force" to get the car moving. Once the car is going, the driver switches to a higher gear. Since it is easier to keep a car moving than to start it moving, the engine can now apply torque to a gear that is smaller in size. At a steady speed, the car can travel with a lower torque. This is because the smaller gear is turning faster. This burns less fuel.

KEY SCIENCE

Engines with a high torque can produce a great amount of force to drive a car. This force can be changed with the use of gears.

Gears are wheels of any size with cogs (teeth) along their rims. The cogs mesh with cogs on other wheels to pass along motion or change speed.

SPEED

Engineers are always trying to improve the speed and performance of cars and motorcycles. Speed records are constantly being smashed, and we are entering the age of the **supersonic** car. That would be a car that can travel faster than the **speed of sound**. Sound travels at more than 1,200 kilometers per hour (km/h), or 750 miles per hour (mph). A supersonic car would travel about 1.6 kilometers (1 mile) every 5 seconds!

Acceleration

Speed is one measure of a high-performance vehicle. **Acceleration** is another. It measures how long it takes for a car to reach 97 km/h (60 mph) from standing still. This graph shows record acceleration rates for some of today's fastest cars and motorcycles.

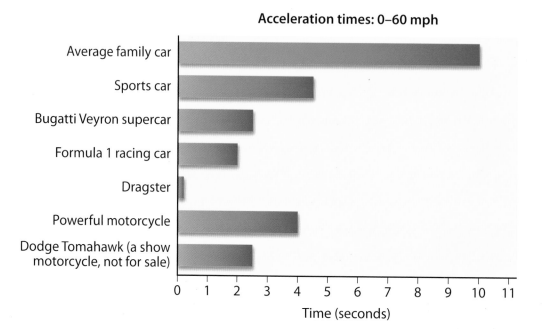

Acceleration times: 0–60 mph

Drag racing

The fastest **accelerating** cars and motorcycles in the world are drag racers. Races are over a short, straight distance of 400 meters (1,300 feet). Vehicles can accelerate (speed up) at an amazing 0–530 km/h (0–330 mph) in only 4.5 seconds. That is 0–97 km/h (0–60 mph) in just 0.2 seconds.

Drag racing became popular 60 years ago in the United States, before it spread around the world. Today, there are hundreds of "dragstrips" where these specialized vehicles roar by at deafening speeds. Races last between 4 and 17 seconds. Finishing speeds range from 130km/h (80 mph) to over 530 km/h (330 mph), depending on the type of vehicle. The fastest ones need parachutes to slow them down and finally "drag" them to a halt.

KEY SCIENCE

Speed is the distance traveled in a certain amount of time.

In other words: Speed = distance ÷ time

A dragster's spinning tires can make a lot of heat and smoke.

Made for speed

A vehicle's shape and weight (**mass**) has a major effect on a vehicle's speed and the amount of fuel it uses. If made with lighter materials and smoother surfaces, cars and motorcycles go faster and need less fuel.

Air wall

Just as a fish swims by pushing through water, vehicles must push through a "wall of air." As the smooth, **streamlined** shape of a fish helps it slip through water easily, so the shape of a car affects how well it moves through air. This is called **aerodynamics**—the study of moving objects through air, and the forces at work on them.

The first cars and motorcycles were built with little thought about their aerodynamics. Today's scientists are always improving designs of vehicles to make them more aerodynamic. The third Law of Motion is the "pushing back" of a vehicle by air, known as **drag**. <u>The faster an object travels, the more drag it experiences</u>.

Vintage race cars have less efficient aerodynamics than modern cars, with their sleek shapes.

Design

Car designers use computer models to test **airflow** (how smoothly air flows around a car). Then, when a vehicle is built, it is tested in a **wind tunnel**. This is a tunnel in which air or smoke is blown over an object. A wind tunnel is where aerodynamics can be scientifically measured.

With modern car designs:

- engineers use rounded shapes to channel air around the vehicle. This gives the least **resistance** (force working against it).

- high-performance cars have features that move air smoothly around, over, and under them.

- a bar called a **spoiler** is sometimes fitted at the back. This stops rushing air from lifting the wheels at high speed. A spoiler works like an upside-down wing. It pushes down and holds the car to the road.

A Porsche GT3 sports car is tested in a wind tunnel. The smoke jets show the airflow.

spoiler

Mega-fast car

The Bloodhound Supersonic Car (SSC) is an extra-fast vehicle. It aims to smash all land speed records and travel at supersonic speeds. This means reaching 1,600 km/h (1,000 mph)! The Bloodhound SSC has wheels made of a metal called **titanium**, which is very light and strong. It has a race car engine just to power its fuel pump, and it uses parachutes as brakes. It is described as the engineering adventure for the future. This British project hopes to inspire young people to think about careers in science, technology, engineering, and mathematics. Interest in these subjects is an important part in this exciting project. The Bloodhound could be the world's fastest car ever.

The challenge

When the Bloodhound is "road tested," it needs a lot of space. The enormous flat landscape of the Hakskeen Pan, in South Africa, is the test site. Any bump on the surface could lift the car off the ground. It will be going so fast that if the aerodynamic design is not exactly right, the car will take off like a plane. It has the same engine as a Eurofighter Typhoon jet plane.

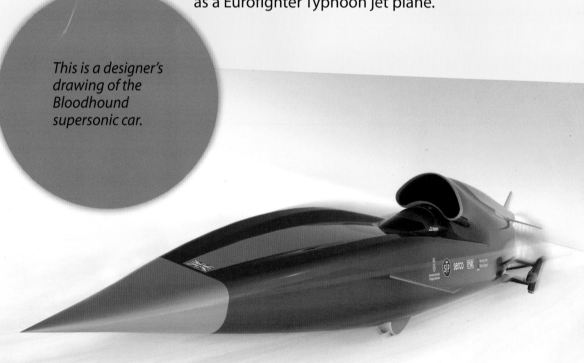

This is a designer's drawing of the Bloodhound supersonic car.

Track record

The large team of engineers at work on the Bloodhound developed the world's first supersonic car in 1997. Named Thrust SSC, it still holds the land speed record of 1,228 km/h (763 mph). Andy Green was its pilot in the Black Rock Desert, in Nevada. He will also be the one to push Bloodhound to its limits. But if you blink, you will miss him!

COMPETITION

The Bloodhound has competition. The North American Eagle is being developed in the United States. Its team of scientists aims "to challenge the current record and bring it back to North America."

KEY SCIENCE

Scientific research involves testing each new invention and idea and all measurable results. That involves a lot of trials, tests, re-tests, and teamwork.

This designer's drawing shows the Bloodhound SSC traveling at supersonic speed.

AUTO RACING

The world of auto racing uses teams of scientists and technology experts to help drivers and riders become winners. The first motor race took place in France in 1894. The winner's average speed was just over 16.4 km/h (10 mph). Today's race cars and motorcycles can go over 320 km/h (200 mph).

FOR THE RECORD

Fastest motorcycle in a race:
The highest speed recorded for a motorcycle is 349 km/h (217 mph). It was reached by Dani Pedrosa riding a Repsol Honda RC212V 800cc at the 2009 Italian motorcycle Grand Prix.

Fastest lap ever in a Formula 1 race car:
Colombian racing driver Juan Pablo Montoya reached a record average speed for a lap at Monza, Italy, in 2004. He was driving a Williams FW27. His average speed was 262 km/h (163 mph).

Juan Pablo Montoya comes in for a stop to change tires during a race in 2010. The crew tries not to waste too much time.

Formula 1 cars

Formula 1 is the highest class of international auto racing. Each car has about 80,000 different parts. The cars can go from 0 to 100 mph (160 km/h) and stop again in 4 seconds. But such power and speed comes at a cost. During a season, a Formula 1 team will use over 200,000 liters (52,800 gallons) of fuel for testing and racing. Each car burns about 200 liters (53 gallons) of fuel in a 300-kilometer (186-mile) race.

DID YOU KNOW?

<u>Formula 1 teams use scientific methods to improve cars' performance and safety</u>. They employ hundreds of people, including scientists. They construct three-dimensional computer models of each race track for testing an engine before each race.

Saving fuel

New engines are being designed to cut the amount of fuel being used in Formula 1 races. But most of the **emissions** (fuel waste in the exhaust gases) in Formula 1 comes from transporting teams and equipment. Powering wind tunnels for testing also uses a lot of fuel. There are plans to reorganize races to cut emissions further.

wing

Wings fitted to a race car actually work like the wings on an aircraft. But they do not lift the car. Instead, they are designed to push it to the road and stop it from "taking off" at high speeds.

GRIP

The whole point of cars and motorcycles is that they move easily. The force that can stop them from doing this is friction. Yet without friction, drivers would be in danger of losing control or never being able to stop.

Even the best race car drivers may lose control under difficult driving conditions.

GOOD OR BAD FRICTION?

Helpful friction: If tires or brakes are badly worn and the road is wet and slippery, the important friction that helps road-holding is lost. Steering and braking is reduced, so there is a higher risk of skidding and crashing.

Harmful friction: Friction inside an engine and on wheel parts will wear down metal. This means that moving parts will no longer work properly. Putting oil or grease on moving parts makes surfaces more slippery and reduces the friction.

Bike science

How do motorcyclists on only two wheels not fall over, especially when speeding around bends?

Friction is both a friend and enemy to the biker. While helping to grip the motorcycle on the bend, friction can also be painful if the motorcycle and rider fall and slide across the road.

With the rider leaning into a bend, friction and various forces keep the motorcycle on the road. If the lean into the bend is too steep, the motorcycle will fall and spin off the road. Anyone falling off a motorcycle soon finds that friction turns into an enemy. Scraping over a road surface can cause clothing materials to burn or melt into wounds. Ouch!

KEY SCIENCE

Friction is what happens when any two surfaces rub against each other. Friction is high if the surfaces are dry and rough. It is low if the surfaces are smooth and wet.

If a rider enters a turn with no lean at all, the motorcycle is likely to fall toward the outside of the turn.

Tires

Riding in a car without tires would be bumpy and unsafe. Tires make for a smooth ride. But their most important job is to hold vehicles on the road and stop them from skidding out of control. Modern tires do this very well. A lot of science goes into their design.

Good tread

Smooth surfaces provide only a little friction. <u>Tires have grooves, ribs, and patterns to help them grip the road in all weather conditions</u>. Grooves do an important job on wet roads by dispersing (moving) water away from the tires. A tire traveling at 95 km/h (60 mph) must disperse over 7.5 liters (2 gallons) of water per second when there are just 3 millimeters (1/10 inch) of water across a road. If this water is not dispersed, the sheet of water can cause tires to lose contact with the road. The car slides on the water, or **aquaplanes**. Worn tires have a reduced ability to disperse water. This makes them skid easily. They are a cause of many accidents.

Engineers make a Mazda RS8 aquaplane on a test track.

KEY SCIENCE

Flooded or oily roads affect a vehicle's traction (grip), because there is less friction between two wet surfaces. Traction is very important for drivers to keep control through corners.

No tread

Not all tires have treads to help traction. In many motor races held in dry conditions, smooth tires are used. These are called **slick** tires. These tires are much wider than normal tires. This means they have a larger surface area in contact with the track. Race cars accelerate and brake at such high speeds that their tires get very hot and sticky. This causes them to grip to the ground, even though they have no tread. But the tires wear out very quickly. This is why they cannot be used for normal road cars.

New slick and wet-surface tires like these are fitted to Formula 1 race cars.

slick tires

wet-surface tires

BRIGHT IDEA: AIR-FILLED TIRES

In 1888 John Dunlop invented air-filled tires. He saw that his son rattled over a bumpy road on a tricycle with solid rubber tires. To make the ride smoother, Dunlop glued rubber tubes around the wheels and pumped them with air. He had invented the first **pneumatic** tire.

Holes in the brake rotor help to disperse the heat.

Brake power

You are racing along in a car, when just ahead someone steps into the road. You slam on the brakes and trust in science! The friction of brake pads against the wheels will hopefully slow you down in time.

Heat

The problem with braking suddenly is that you must quickly get rid of all that energy from moving (called kinetic energy). The energy turns into heat as motion is slowed down. That means brakes soon get red hot—up to temperatures of 500 °C (950 °F). <u>Brakes today are made from materials that won't melt, such as alloys (mixtures of metals) or **ceramics**</u>. Ceramics are special materials. Unlike brakes in the past, ceramics can withstand very high temperatures.

Life-saving science

If you look at a car's wheels, you can often see a shiny metal disc inside. This is the **brake rotor**. By pressing on the brake pedal, a driver clamps a pad onto this rotor. The rubbing slows the vehicle down. This science uses the energy from the driver's foot and sends it with great force to all brake pads.

Hydraulic systems use fluid-filled pipes. The fluid increases the force many times over and transfers it from one place to another. This is how the driver's foot can instantly apply great friction onto all brake rotors and stop the heavy car in seconds.

BRIGHT IDEA: HYDRAULIC BRAKES

In 1918 U.S. engineer Malcolm Lougheed invented hydraulic brakes. He used cylinders and tubes to apply fluid pressure against the wheels. This slowed them down. His new hydraulic brakes were not popular immediately. During the 1920s, car makers began to use his brake design. But the huge car company Ford did not use his invention until 1939. Lougheed changed his name to "Lockheed," and with his brother Allan, he started the famous Lockheed Aircraft Corporation.

This diagram shows how hydraulic brakes work.

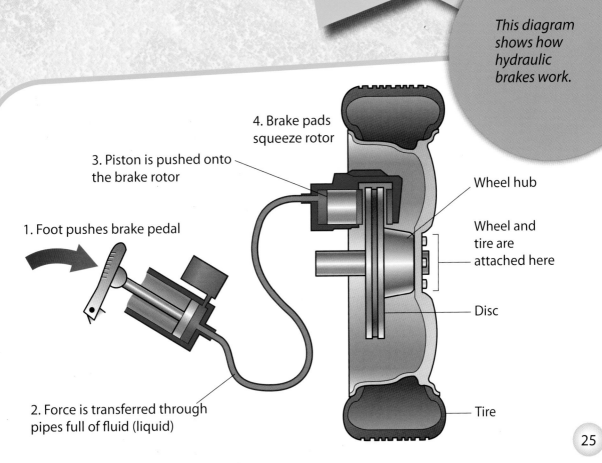

3. Piston is pushed onto the brake rotor

4. Brake pads squeeze rotor

1. Foot pushes brake pedal

2. Force is transferred through pipes full of fluid (liquid)

Wheel hub

Wheel and tire are attached here

Disc

Tire

CRASH SCIENCE

When brakes fail to stop a vehicle in time, the resulting crash releases all its remaining energy. Scientists often have to investigate the crash site like detectives. They use the evidence left behind to see what happened.

Crash detectives

"Crash scientists" are called **forensic** investigators. One kind of evidence they examine is friction—in the form of skid marks. From their length, direction, and the amounts of tread left behind on the road and on the tires, these experts can figure out the speed at which the vehicle was traveling.

Forensic investigators work to understand crashes like this one at a Formula 1 race in 2010.

Speed and braking distances

A car speeding at 112 km/h (70 mph) will obviously take longer to stop than a car going at half that speed. You can see from the chart below that it takes almost 100 meters (328 feet) for a car going at 112 km/h (70 mph) to stop. About 20 meters (66 feet) of that distance is just "thinking time," while the driver reacts before slamming on the brakes. The supersonic car Thrust SSC, with its land speed record of 1228 km/h (763 mph), has a total stopping distance of about 10 kilometers (6 miles)!

KEY SCIENCE

A car or motorcycle crashing at speed results in a lot of friction and a sudden release of kinetic energy.

The greater the speed, the greater the energy (and the greater the likelihood of damage on impact).

This graph shows braking distances at different speeds. Braking distance is increased by poor road conditions (for example, icy or wet roads) and poor car conditions (for example, bald tires, poor brakes, or too many people).

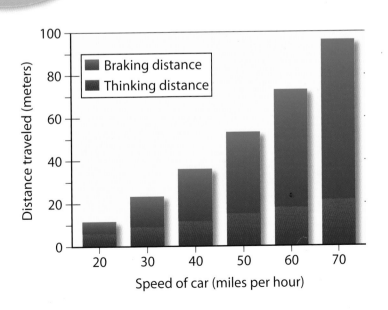

Super safe

Scientists are always researching new and better ways to keep drivers, motorcyclists, and passengers safe in the event of a crash. Their work on how best to absorb "crash energy" has been effective in saving lives.

Cars used to be made of solid steel. This was thought to protect everyone in a crash. But passengers were often hurt by the massive force of impact, since there was nothing to absorb the crash energy. In the 1950s, cars began to be made with a high-strength steel safety cage, but with **crumple zones**, too. These are areas at the front and the rear of a car that are designed to absorb the crash. <u>Car designs with crumple zones that buckle easily spread the crash forces over a large area of the car</u>. Just 1 meter (3.3. feet) of crumpled car can cut much of the force reaching passengers inside.

Crashing a sedan at a research center helps scientists study "crash science."

CRASH SCIENCE

How would you like a job where you crash cars and motorcycles all day? Crash scientists do just that. They use measuring equipment on vehicles and dummies, recording each detail in slow motion. In this way, they can design crumple zones and airbags for absorbing crash energy and protecting people.

Airbags

In the 1990s, gas-inflated airbags had to be fitted in all new cars. This was after a lot of crash research went into making them effective. An airbag inflates at a speed of up to 124 km/h (200 mph) within one twenty-fifth of a second. That force creates an instant cushion to absorb energy and help protect people's body parts.

The world's first motorcycle airbag was demonstrated by Honda in 2005.

BRIGHT IDEA: AIRBAGS IN A JACKET

The Honda company developed an airbag that was attached to the front of a motorcycle. Next came airbags attached to the rider! A jacket with an airbag inside is blasted with compressed air when a cord rips out if the rider falls. In an instant, the jacket inflates to cushion the fall and reduce the impact and possible injury.

AT THE CUTTING EDGE

Some of the latest science and technology research is aimed at developing amazing vehicle performance. Recent cutting-edge electronics have produced breathtaking advances for both drivers and bikers.

Intelligent cars

Car makers are now working on how cars "think." One area of research is a Danger Lookout System in the form of a "smart camera." This warns drivers of accident risks on the road ahead.

Israel's General Motors research team is developing a computer vision system to make cars smarter and roads safer. A camera with a powerful microchip (a tiny part of a computer) is able to notice the behavior of people and animals ahead. It then prompts the car to brake, swerve, or even lock the doors.

The LIFEcar is called a **"zero emission"** (non-polluting) sports car. It has a top speed of nearly 160 km/h (100 mph). It runs on a light gas called **hydrogen** and can accelerate from 0 to 60 miles (96 km) in just 7 seconds.

Auto steering

Other computer vision technology being developed at North Carolina State University can control a car's steering. It can keep the vehicle in the right lane, avoid traffic, and react to emergencies—such as when a driver has fallen asleep at the wheel. But maybe the driver is more likely to fall asleep if the car does all the thinking!

SUPER CAR

If you have about $1.6 million to spend on a car, you might like the Bugatti Veyron. It is probably the most expensive new road car you can buy. Its top speed is 430 km/h (268 mph). In 2010 it was declared the fastest car on the road. From standing still, it takes just 15 seconds to reach 300 km/h (186 mph). But if you zoom along at 400 km/h (250 mph) for more than 12 minutes, you will run out of fuel. It is probably for the best. After 25 minutes at that speed, the tires are likely to catch fire. So might the brakes, as it can squeal to a stop from that top speed in just 10 seconds!

A Bugatti Veyron stunned people on the streets of France in 2009. It was the 100th anniversary of the Bugatti company.

Superbikes

The Mission Motor Company of San Francisco, California, produced an electric superbike called Mission One. It was the first to break a land speed record of over 240 km/h (150 mph). The superbike broke the fastest electric vehicle record on the Bonneville Salt Flats in Utah in 2009. It gave out no harmful carbon dioxide gases. This is because this superbike is battery powered and has only one gear.

Green clean machine

Mission One 2010 is powered by high-energy **lithium-ion batteries** (see box on page 33). These can hold three times more energy than batteries of 10 years ago, which then cost twice as much. The Mission One engineers tell how their latest motorcycle can even recycle some of its energy: "It recaptures the kinetic energy of the motorcycle during braking and turns it into **electrical energy**." Electrical energy is stored in batteries.

By recapturing this energy, the Mission One can go farther on a single charge. When the batteries run out, the rider just charges the motorcycle again from an ordinary wall outlet. Filling up the motorcycle from empty only costs about two dollars.

The Mission One motorcycle has a top speed of 240 km/h (150 mph) and an estimated range of 240 km (150 miles).

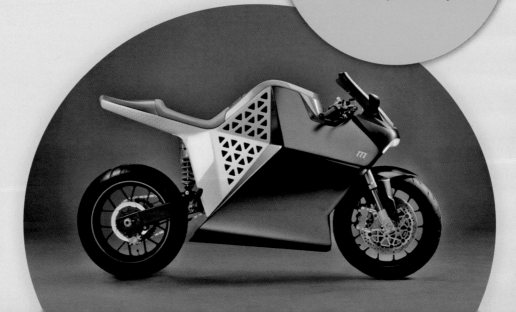

Is it a bike, is it a car, is it a rocket?

In 2009 the world's fastest motorcycle was put through its paces on the Bonneville Salt Flats. It reached 590 km/h (367.382 mph). That's like traveling the length of five football fields in 3.3 seconds! The team of engineers developed the BUB Seven Streamliner's shape using a wind tunnel. It scored the lowest amount of drag ever recorded. The crew plans to break the world speed record again.

DID YOU KNOW?

Lithium is the lightest metal. It is soft enough to cut with scissors. It easily floats on water, reacting by moving around and releasing hydrogen. Lithium-ion batteries are generally smaller and lighter than other batteries. They are more powerful, too, and hold their charge longer. <u>Lithium-ion batteries tend to cost a lot of money. Research is under way to make them cheaper and stronger.</u>

This is the BUB Seven Streamliner being tested in a wind tunnel.

FUTURE TECHNOLOGY

Today's developing technology will create very different cars and motorcycles in the next 50 years, let alone by the next century. We are about to see many changes in how vehicles will work.

Environmentally friendly

The big change in vehicle technology is already happening. We are moving from gas-guzzling engines to cleaner vehicles that use less fuel. The world's oil cannot last forever. Different ways of running cars and motorcycles have to be found.

More vehicles are being made that run on hydrogen. Hydrogen is a **renewable** fuel, which means it will not run out. This is because it can be extracted (taken) from water. The only emission from exhaust is harmless water vapor. Vehicles can use **fuel cells** to change the hydrogen into electricity. A fuel cell, like a battery, creates electricity, but it needs gas or liquid fuel to make it work. This is still expensive, and there are technical challenges. The science is developing all the time to overcome them.

This Japanese electric motorcycle can go over 100 miles (160 kilometers) on one charge.

Green technology

Hybrid vehicles still use a gasoline engine. They also have an electric motor powered by batteries. The batteries are charged by energy from the moving wheels and from the brakes. This has a good environmental impact for the following reasons.

• A hybrid car's battery can last for around 200,000 miles (320,000 kilometers). This is much longer than a normal car battery.

• At present, hybrid cars need about 30 percent less gasoline than normal cars.

• A computer controls the power needed from the gasoline engine and the electric engine. The computer regulates them to be very fuel efficient.

ENVIRONMENTAL IMPACT

Some of the latest cars use renewable and recycled materials. They can be described as **sustainable** (capable of continuing to work without harming the environment). The world's first sustainable race car runs on waste chocolate! The car has a top speed of 215 km/h (135 mph) and can go from 0 to 60 mph (97 km/h) in 2.5 seconds.

The WorldF3rst Formula 3 race car was made in the United Kingdom in 2009.

Extreme cars

Is it a bird? Is it a fish? It's a car! Technology is making it possible for cars to adapt as never before. Maybe the very rare machines already out there might soon become part of everyday life.

Takeoff

If you have a spare $200,000 and a pilot's license, you could have your own flying car. The new vehicle, made by the Terrafugia Company, is called Transition. Terrafugia call it "the greenest plane in the sky." That's because it flies using normal gasoline at about 20 liters (5 gallons) per hour.

If you are going for a drive and there is a holdup ahead, you just need several hundred feet of road for takeoff. Simply unfold the wings and you are in the sky. Or you could get into your other car and head for the beach for an underwater adventure…

The Terrafugia Transition is called a "roadable aircraft."

Going under

The Swiss Rinspeed sQuba is the world's first zero-emission electric sports car that can be driven underwater. It has three electric motors. One is for land travel and two are for water. The car has an open top to allow the driver and passenger to escape in an emergency. It can dive 10 meters (33 feet) under the sea.

The Aquada is just right for vacations by the sea!

A SPLASH OF SUPER SCIENCE

The Aquada sports car can reach up to 160 km/h (100 mph) on land, before driving down the beach and on to the sea. At the press of a button, it uses a jet to propel it through the waves. The wheels automatically rise. Then, as you press the accelerator, the thrust (force) pushes the car at over 50 km/h (30 mph) over the water. The Aquada's makers specialize in high-speed land-and-water vehicles. This includes the Quadski quad bike, which skims over the ocean at a breathtaking 72 km/h (50 mph).

TOMORROW'S WORLD

Research is already well under way to make vehicles that can drive themselves. It may still seem like science fiction, but scientists are developing the technology to let you type in the address of where you want to go. Your car or motorcycle will then take you there cleanly and silently, as you sit back and enjoy the view.

"We think the car of the future could be drawing power from its roof, its hood or even the door, thanks to our new material. Even the **Sat Nav** [satellite navigator] could be powered by its own casing."

Dr. Emile Greenhalgh, Imperial College London

This driverless car is being developed in Stanford, California. It has a monitor in the backseat to display information.

SATELLITE TECHNOLOGY

Global Positioning System (**GPS**) engineers are developing more ways to improve safety. Three-dimensional modeling technology used in many advanced GPS devices can warn drivers of dangerous turns and obstacles in the road long before the vehicle is near. A red light comes on inside the car or an alarm sounds to alert the driver. At the same time, the Sat Nav gets to work redirecting the driver to avoid problems ahead.

Self-powering

Hybrid cars and motorcycles are certain to develop further, but so are **tribrids**. Tribids use three forms of energy. In addition to a fuel engine and an electric motor, power comes from other sources of energy, such as **solar** (Sun) **power** or wind power. The 2010 Toyota Prius already uses **solar panels** to supply some of its power needs. Solar panels are devices that turn sunlight into electrical energy. More amazingly, <u>parts of a car's bodywork may soon supply much of its power</u>. Researchers in London, England, are working on lightweight materials that store and release electrical energy.

So, back to that question: What would the world be like without cars and motorcycles? Maybe you can now imagine tomorrow's world, where scientists create some very different vehicles for that exciting road ahead.

TIMELINE

1769	The first self-propelled steam car is built by Nicolas Cugnot in France for the French army.
1869	The first bicycle powered with a steam engine—the first motorcycle—is built in France.
1885/86	The first cars and motorcycles are built using internal combustion engines. They are built by two engineers working in separate parts of Germany—Gottlieb Daimler and Karl Benz.
1899	The first police car is built by Collins Buggy Company. It is powered by an electric battery.
EARLY 1900s	Henry Ford (1863–1947) begins mass-producing cars, despite warnings from his money manager not to do so.
1903	The Harley Davidson motorcycle company starts in the United States. The same year the motorcycle sidecar is invented.
1914	Ford's Michigan car factory takes just 93 minutes to make a complete Model T car. More than half the world's cars are Model T Fords.
1938	The Volkswagen Beetle car is first produced. (The last was produced in 2003.)
1948	The Honda motorcycle company is formed in Japan. Today, Honda is the world's largest manufacturer of motorcycles and the world's largest manufacturer of internal combustion engines.
1965	Controls on harmful vehicle carbon emissions are introduced in California, with the rest of the world soon doing the same.

1980s	Anti-lock brakes are fitted to many new cars. They use computerized sensors to adjust braking pressures and prevent the wheels from "locking up" and skidding in emergency braking.
1988	BMW introduces the first motorcycle with an electronic-hydraulic ABS (anti-lock braking system).
1999	Honda and Toyota introduce the first modern gasoline/electric hybrid cars in Japan, then in the United States and Europe in 2002.
2005	Fuel-cell technology is used in the making of some electric motorcycles.
2006	The Aston Martin DB5 used in the James Bond movies *Goldfinger* and *Thunderball* is sold for over $4 million. The car's gadgets include built-in Browning machine guns, tire-slashers, and an oil slick ejector.
2009	The Mission One superbike becomes the fastest electric-powered vehicle, with an average speed of 241.5 km/h (150 mph) over 2 miles.
2011	The Transition flying car goes on sale in the United States.
2012	Honda and Nissan are to begin mass-producing electric cars for the global market. Among the options will be a mid-size to large plug-in hybrid and an all-electric model.
2013	New engine designs for Formula 1 are to be in place to cut fuel use by almost 50 percent.

Quiz

1

Isaac Newton's first Law of Motion is

a) the faster you go, the colder you get

b) you will keep moving at the same speed in the same direction unless a force acts on you

c) if you free-wheel downhill without any brakes, you need gears to help you stop

2

Combustion is a chemical reaction that occurs

a) between a fuel and oxygen

b) between sunlight and carbon

c) between water and hydrogen

3

3. Acceleration is an increase in

a) thermal energy

b) speed

c) torque

4

Two surfaces rubbing together cause

a) friction and heat

b) burns and blisters

c) smoke and skids

5

A car or motorcycle crashing at speed results in a sudden release of

a) tension

b) kinetic energy

c) gas

6

Modern race cars have wings

a) to make them look really cool

b) to help them fly over the car in front

c) to improve the airflow that helps them hold onto the road

8

Electric superbikes like Mission One 2010 are powered by

a) hydrogen

b) lithium-ion batteries

c) solar panels

9

A hybrid vehicle

a) can go on land and water

b) is powered by a fuel engine and an electric motor

c) is recycled and has zero emissions

7

Modern car designs have crumple zones to

a) absorb crash energy

b) help aerodynamics

c) improve fuel consumption

10

The streamlined shape of race cars and motorcycles is to cut down

a) drag

b) mass

c) heat

Glossary

accelerate speed up

acceleration act of speeding up; also, a measurement of how long it takes to speed up

aerodynamics study of motion and forces of air on an object

airflow how smoothly air flows around a car

aquaplane to rise over a thin film of water between a car's tires and the road

biofuel fuel made from living things or the waste they produce

brake rotor shiny metal disc inside a car's wheel that helps slow a vehicle down

ceramic strong and hard material made by heating non-metallic minerals at high temperatures

combustion burning fuel with oxygen, which releases energy as well as gases and polluting particles

compress squeeze or crush

crankshaft part of an engine that rotates to carry power from pistons to the gearbox, then to the wheels

crumple zone area at the front and back of a car designed to buckle in a crash and be a shock absorber

cylinder one of the tube-shaped parts inside an engine where fuel is burned to make energy. A car engine can have between two and twelve cylinders.

drag force from air resistance as a vehicle travels at speed

electrical energy energy made by the flow of an electric charge

emission fuel waste in the exhaust gases of cars

energy ability to produce movement or activity, or to do work

engineer person who uses math and science to design useful products

exhaust escaping gas or vapor

force push or pull that makes an object speed up, slow down, change direction, or change shape

forensic using scientific methods to investigate and establish facts in criminal courts

four-stroke engine internal combustion engine that follows four strokes, or steps: 1.) an explosive mixture is drawn into the cylinder; 2.) it is compressed; 3.) it is ignited; 4.) exhaust gases are released

friction rubbing force when two surfaces come into contact and move against each other

fuel cell device that changes the chemical energy of a fuel (usually hydrogen) directly into electrical energy

gear wheel with cogs (teeth) around its rim

Global Positioning System (GPS) system that tracks the exact position of a vehicle

hybrid vehicle with two power sources: a gasoline engine and a rechargeable battery-powered motor

hydraulic system science of using moving liquid, such as water through tubes, to transmit energy

hydrogen light, invisible gas that can be burned and used for power in a fuel cell

kinetic energy energy of motion

lithium-ion battery type of small, light battery that is very powerful and holds its charge for a long time

lubrication keeping parts running smoothly by using substances like oil

mass amount of matter that something contains

mass-produce make in large quantities

performance in cars, the ability to speed up

piston plunger that fits tightly inside an engine cylinder, moving up and down as the fuel combusts

pneumatic made to be filled with compressed air

renewable describes sources that will not run out. For example, biofuel can be made from plants or animal waste.

resistance force that works against the movement of objects

Sat Nav satellite navigation system

slick type of tire that has no tread pattern, used mostly in auto racing

solar panel grid of connected cells that collects sunlight and changes it into electrical energy

solar power useful energy captured from sunlight

speed of sound speed at which sound travels. This is about 1,193 km/h (332 mph), but it can vary with temperature and height above the ground.

spoiler bar fitted at the back of a car, it stops rushing air from lifting the wheels at high speed

streamlined rounded, smooth design of a vehicle that improves its speed by reducing drag

supersonic above the speed of sound

sustainable capable of continuing to work without harming the environment

thrust pushing force that moves a vehicle

titanium silvery-gray light, strong metal

torque force that produces twisting

traction friction of an object moving on a surface, giving grip (such as a tire)

tribrid vehicle with three power sources: an engine, a battery-powered motor, and solar panels

wind tunnel chamber in which air or smoke is blown over an object to help measure its aerodynamic forces

zero emission causing no significant pollution from exhaust gases

Find Out More

Books

Hammond, Richard. *Car Science*. New York: Dorling Kindersley, 2008.

Nixon, James. *Machines on the Move: Motorcycles*. Mankato, Minn.: Amicus, 2011.

Oxlade, Chris. *Machines Inside Out: Motorcycles*. New York: Rosen/PowerKids, 2009.

Parker, Steve. *How it Works: Cars, Trucks, and Bikes*. Broomall, Pa.: Mason Crest, 2011.

Williams, Brian. *Breakthroughs in Science and Technology: Who Invented the Automobile?* Mankato, Minn.: Arcturus, 2010.

Websites

North American Eagle: Supersonic Land Speed Challenger
www.landspeed.com/index.htm

BrainPOP Technology: Learn About Cars
www.brainpop.com/technology/transportation/cars/preview.weml

The Science Behind Bloodhound
www.impactworld.org.uk/casevideos.php?vid=3

Car Smarts: Car Safety
http://auto.howstuffworks.com/car-driving-safety/safety-regulatory-devices/car-safety-quiz.htm

How Motorcycles Work
http://auto.howstuffworks.com/motorcycle.htm

Automobile Timeline
www.greatachievements.org/?id=3880

Topics for further research

- Electric vehicles of the 1800s

- Speed and G-force

- Types of car and motorcycle racing

- The strangest cars and motorcycles ever invented (there were quite a few)

- Future fuels and sources of energy.

Index